Twitter Power!

Written For Web Sites Depot

By

Randolph M. Hirsch

Moshe Publications, Inc.

Disclaimer

The publisher has made every effort to be as accurate and complete as possible in this report, notwithstanding the fact that he does not warrant or represent at any time that the contents within are accurate due to the rapidly changing nature of the Internet.

While all attempts have been made to verify information in this report, the publisher accepts no responsibility for errors, omissions or contrary interpretation of the subject matter within. Any perceived slights of specific persons, peoples or organizations are unintentional.

This book is a step by step guide to generating free traffic. In practical advice books like this there is no guarantee of results, traffic or income. Readers are cautioned to rely on their own judgement about their individual circumstances and abilities to act accordingly.

This book is not intended to be used as a source of legal, business, accounting or financial advice. All readers are encouraged to seek services of competent professionals in the legal, business, accounting and financial fields.

Table of Contents

Introduction

Twitter is what is known as a micro-blogging platform. Instead of posting full length blog posts you have just 140 characters to make your post.

Now this can be a challenge and we will talk about this in a little while, but you have to fit your posts into this apparently small number of characters.

Recent figures from research firm Nielsen Online show that visitors to the site increased by 1,382%, from 475,000 to seven million, between February 2008 and February 2009. It is thought to have grown beyond 40 million since then.

This study discovered majority of people who use Twitter only ever Tweet a few times, though those that do post, post prolifically. The Internet Marketing community is, of course, particularly active on Twitter.

                   http://www.websitesdesignla.com

Twitter really is a broadcast medium, i.e. you broadcast your posts into the system rather than a system like Facebook or Myspace which is much more intimate and involved.

A whole terminology has grown up around Twitter, with almost it's on language. This can be very confusing to the newcomer, but this book will explain all of the terms that are commonly used as we go along.

Posting to Twitter.com is called "Tweeting". A post to Twitter is called a Tweet. The language is kind of cute really, with a whole sub-culture developing around dedicated Twitterers (or Tweets).

If you are using Twitter for building your business, which we will assume you are as you are reading this book then you need to pay attention to what you Tweet ... more of that in the next section.

Twitter has grown massively in popularity over the last couple of years and has assumed almost cult status with many celebrities and businesses jumping on to the bandwagon.

The basic principle is that you post your Tweets and your followers read them. You build up followers over time by searching and finding people with similar interests. You follow them and in many cases they will follow you back.

You are also found by people who follow you and you can follow them back to.

It's effectively a mini social network. You can send and receive direct messages (limited to 140 characters) to other people on Twitter, though a lot of the time these are ignored as many people abuse the direct message system and spam.

The only downside of Twitter is that if you follow a lot of people or a couple of celebrities you can find there is an awful lot of noise on your Twitter account from their posts.

Jonathan Ross, a UK TV presenter is well known for posting tens or hundreds of Tweets within an hour – he uses Twitter to communicate with his fans and to promote his shows. In fact he gave away a trip to the US to meet a major pop star to one of his Twitter followers.

Because Jonathan posts so much, many of the other Tweets you may want to read get pushed down

If you are planning on using Twitter for business and personal usage then I would recommend you set up two different accounts. Much like the other social networks, your personal Tweeting will get lost in all the noise from the marketers.

This program has been designed to help you get the most from Twitter and to understand how to use it to not only build your business but to establish yourself as an expert and an authority in your chosen field.

Twitter is a valuable tool for marketers to establish themselves as experts in their field and to make people aware of their products and services. Through Twitter you can help to give your reputation and your business a boost.

Signing Up To Twitter

Signing up to Twitter is free and easy to do. All you need to do is go to www.Twitter.com and click on the Getting Started – Join button.

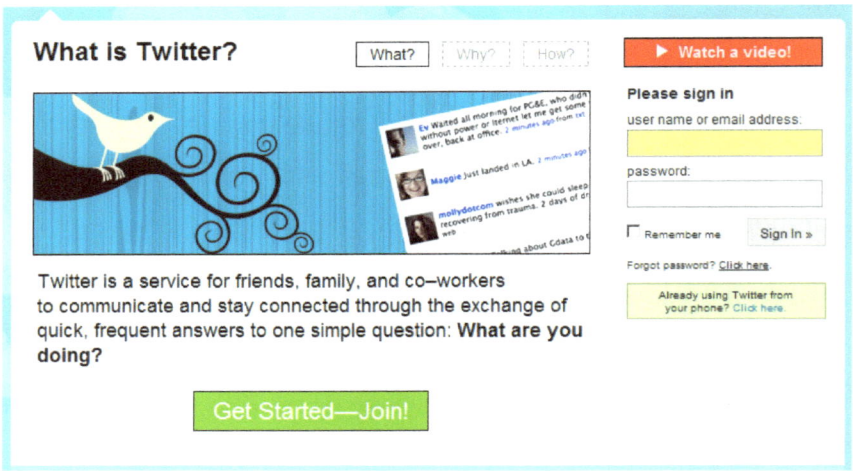

The sign up process is very simple. Just complete the form, making sure you include a valid email address so that you can reset your password if you have to in the future.

One of the main questions on this form is what should you use as your Twitter username.

Your Twitter username is very important. People who are coming to your Twitter account will go to www.twitter.com/yourTwitterName. This means that they will see your twitter name.

There is a debate raging about whether you should use your keywords or your name.

The answer to that question is … it depends.

It depends on what you are using Twitter for. If you are using Twitter to build your reputation as an expert then you need to use your name.

If you are using Twitter for SEO purposes or for a specific website, then keywords may be best.

The picture below shows you the sign up form that you need to complete. You can see it is very easy!

Join the Conversation

Already use Twitter on your phone? Finish signup now.

Already on Twitter? Sign in

Full name [   ] enter your first and last name

Username

Your URL: http://twitter.com/USERNAME

Password

Email

☐ I want the inside scoop—please send me email updates!

aryahs   Harlems

Can't read this?
↻ Get two new words
◄ Listen to the words
Powered by reCAPTCHA
Help

Type the words above

Create my account

Once you are signed up to Twitter you need to start Tweeting (see the next section) and update your profile and bio.

This is so that people can find you when they search on Twitter and so that people who find you can find out a bit more about you before they follow you. This will ensure you build a very relevant list of followers.

On the main account settings page, you need to add some settings.

Firstly, put in a URL. Rather than putting this as a sales page (you may do if you are specifically on Twitter to sell) you may want to put this to a blog or other information site that further builds your reputation and establishes you as an expert.

Next you have to a 160 character bio. This is a brief bio of you and what you do. Make sure this is keyword rich but readable for real people. This is a very important field as it is used by Twitter when people perform searches.

Due to the limitation in characters you need to be concise. Something like marketer, speaker, businessman, programmer for example. Separate out your keywords with commas rather than trying to make a complete sentence – you will get more into the 160 characters they give you!

Also it is worth putting in your location as this will help people who are geographically close to you locate you, which can be very beneficial.

The picture below shows you these settings.

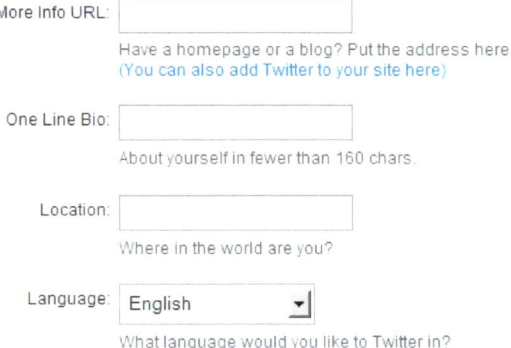

If you are planning on Tweeting in a language other than English, then you will want to change the final setting here. This is useful if you are targeting users in a specific country.

The big question is do you have multiple Twitter accounts for every website and niche your work in or just one main account.

The best way to operate is to have a number of different Twitter accounts for each general niche.

For example, you would have one for dog training rather than one for individual breed dog training or for different types of training.

The rationale behind this is that if your focus is too broad then you will be sending out irrelevant messages to the majority of your Twitter followers. This will confuse them and may lead them to stop following you.

Remember you want a targeted followers list and if the focus of your Twitter account is too broad you won't be able to meet their needs properly.

Tweeting On Twitter

Posting on Twitter is simply a case of writing 140 characters in a box and pressing the update button.

What are you doing?

Latest: Just posting here on Twitter to say Howdy folks less than 5 seconds ago

update

The real key to succeeding with Twitter is knowing what to post and what not to post.

If you are using Twitter for business and for building your reputation as an authority figure, then you need to be very careful about what you post. Don't make inane posts like, "Going to make a cup of tea" or "Reading the newspaper".

Make sure that every post counts and establishes you as an expert – remember people can read every Tweet that you make – another reason for you to separate out your personal and business Twitter accounts.

         http://www.websitesdesignla.com

The good thing about Twitter is the character limitation forces you to be concise and to think about what you are posting. Many marketers use Twitter to advertise their products and services and some use it to provide tips on their specialist niche.

The latter can be a challenge to fit something meaningful into just 140 characters, but it does make you really think about what you are posting.

Twitter is very good for creating a buzz about a new product launch or advertising an existing product or service. If you have a loyal group of followers then you can use Twitter to get them excited about the new launch so that they will buy.

Twitter can be used to educate your followers to the benefits of your product / service so that they understand why it is they must have it.

If you are doing this, then you will find it much easier to plan out your Tweets first so that you have a coherent campaign. You may add messages to it based on feedback and questions that you get from your followers, but the plan will make it easier in the long run.

Twitter is also a very good platform for keeping your followers updated on development work or for notifications. For example, the LA Fire Department use Twitter to keep people informed of local fire emergencies. Some Internet Marketers use Twitter to keep people informed of new products. Some companies use Twitter to inform people of special offers and new stock.

The use of Twitter is only limited by your imagination. The more unique your approach to using it then the more likely you are to get a good result from it.

If you look for other experts in your field who are Tweeting and see what they are doing it will give you an idea of what is working. If you then take this and improve on it then you will do even better.

Whenever you Tweet you need to focus on one thing and one thing only.

And it's not the sale.

You need to focus on the click through.

Even the greatest marketer will struggle to sell a product in 140 characters. It may be possible, but will not be easy.

However, if instead you focus on education people to the benefits of your product or service and focus on the click through to your website then you will find you get much better results.

Once you have people on your website, then you can focus on the more traditional methods of selling and marketing to them.

Tweeting can be a nerve-wracking experience, you are posting something that real people will see and read! For some this is a very frightening prospect.

If you do post something you regret or want to delete don't panic, you can do that. Go to your updates and hold your mouse over the post you want to delete. You will see a small trash icon appear.

Simply click on that and your post will be gone.

keyword rich post with your URL in this case http://www.google.com

12:10 PM Jun 19th from web

The star, by the way, allows you to mark it as a favorite so that you can easily find the Tweet again in the future if you need to.

Working With Followers

Followers are a vital component of working with Twitter. Followers are people who have expressed an interest in you and your Tweets and are following you.

This means that whenever you make a Tweet, it automatically appears on their Twitter home page.

If they have a lot of followers or followers who are particularly vocal on Twitter then you may find that your message disappears fairly quickly off the screen. This is why many marketers will post the same or similar messages a number of times to ensure maximum readership.

Home

 Wossy On tonights show. Mitchell and webb, Matthew fox, Davina
and Rev and the Makers !http://twitpic.com/7sgm3
1 minute ago from TweetDeck

 John_Taylor Dedicated to all Mothers.. in the Pink.. ♫
http://blip.fm/~8hyyv
27 minutes ago from Blip.fm

 John_Taylor What else would you listen to on Friday? ;-) ♫
http://blip.fm/~8hyu1
33 minutes ago from Blip.fm

 John_Taylor Free affiliate marketing training.. http://affiliate-
marketing-...
35 minutes ago from TweetDeck

You can see from the above screen shot just a few of the messages that you get when you follow people. Some are relevant, some are not so important.

You can see here that some Twitterers are very prolific in their postings, the two that are featured in the picture above often make a lot of Tweets all at once.

In order to find people to follow and who will hopefully follow you back you need to click on the Find People link in the top right hand corner.

Home Profile Find People Settings Help Sign out

From here you have a number of different options:

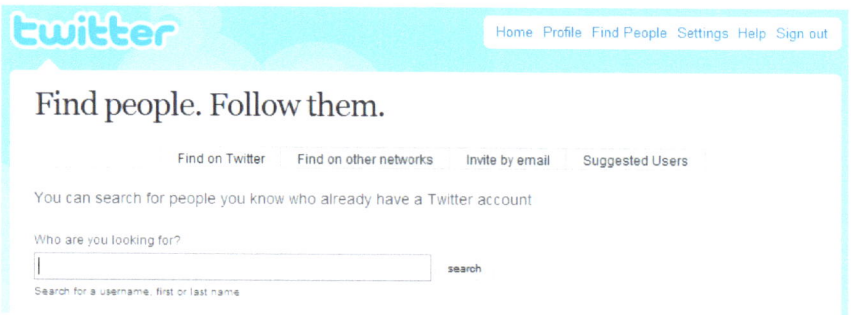

You can search for people directly on Twitter, find them on other social networks or invite people from your email address book to join.

The final option is suggested users. These are users who Twitter thinks may be of interest to you. These often aren't particularly relevant, but it's the thought that counts and you can usually find a few people to follow.

People you follow will often, but not always, follow you back.

In order to maximize your followers you need to make sure your Tweets are keyword rich. They have to contain keywords that people will use to search for information in Twitter.

This is important because the other way of finding followers on Twitter is to put a keyword in the search box and look for Tweets relating to that keyword.

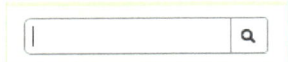

This will then bring up a big list of related Tweets and you can look through them to find people that you will want to follow. Again, hopefully some of these will convert into followers for you. This reverse following is particularly popular in the Internet Marketing field as marketers want to see what other people are up to.

This is why it is so important that your Tweets are keyword rich and based around information people in your niche will want to hear. Don't sacrifice quality of a Tweet in order to shoe horn some keywords in. Always go for quality of Tweeting first with keywords a second. Remember, it is real people that are reading your Tweets, not just a search engine.

There are software tools you can buy that will automate adding followers for you. These always walk a fine line against violating the terms of service and if you are discovered using one that Twitter doesn't approve of you will find your account disabled and deleted instantly.

My personal approach is to avoid these tools as there is too much risk in loosing your account and you have no control over which followers are actually added. It is better for you to have 100 highly targeted followers rather than 1,000 random strangers following you.

The manual approach may take more time but you will end up with a better quality of follower. Look to add around 50-100 people a day. Add many more than that and Twitter may start to get a bit twitchy!

Twitter And Wordpress

Wordpress is a very powerful piece of software that you can not only use for blogs but is useful for pretty much any type of website you can think of. More and more marketers are moving their operations to Wordpress because it is a much more hands free operation and has some very powerful features.

One that is of interest to us here is it can be easily integrated with Twitter.

You can add new functionality to Wordpress through what is known as a plugin. This is a small software tool written by a Wordpress user or marketer that extends the functionality of Wordpress and adds new features or improves existing ones.

There are thousands of different plugins available, but there are around 60 that are related to Twitter. They all do similar things in allowing Twitter and Wordpress to interact with each other.

The screenshot on the next page shows just some of the available plugins.

When looking for a plugin to use you need to look at the rating. Don't just look at the rating, hold your mouse over the rating to see how many ratings it has had.

It is much better to have a slightly lower rating and a high number of ratings that a rating of 5 based on 1 rating.

Name	Version	Rating	Description
Twitter Tools	1.6	★★★★☆	Twitter Tools is a plugin that creates a complete integration between your WordPress blog and your Twitter account. By Alex King.
Twitter Sharts	0.3.2	★☆☆☆☆	'Shart' your twitter status anywhere within your wordpress blog posts or pages! Configure Twitter Sharts By bboyredcel.
Twitter for Wordpress	1.9.4	★★★★★	Twitter for WordPress displays yours latest tweets in your WordPress blog. Features * Simply * Customizable * Widget support * No options page (yes, its a feature) * Uses Wordpress resources (no extra files needed) * Detects URLs, e-mail address and @username replies Usage If you use WordPress widgets, just drag the widget into your sidebar and configure. If widgets are not your thing, ... By Ricardo González.
Twitter Widget	1.0.3	★★★★☆	Adds a sidebar widget to display Twitter updates (uses the Javascript Twitter 'badge') By Sean Spalding.
Elegant Twitter Widget	1.0b	★☆☆☆☆	A WordPress widget that displays twitter updates in yummy valid semantic XHTML code. The code is heavily commented and the output is in template functions so everything is fully customizable. In this version, the plugin grabs the XML twitter feed and parses it using the PHP XML parser, instead of SimpleXML, to support PHP 4. By Paul Shen.
Twitter This	1.0	★★★☆☆	Allow to your readers sharing your blog post at twitter. By Andres Artux Scheffer.
Twitter Widget Pro	1.3.7	★★★★☆	A widget that properly handles twitter feeds, including @username, #hashtag, and link parsing. It supports displaying profiles images, and even lets you control whether to display the time and date of a tweet or how log ago it happened

As you can see from the above picture there are a lot of different plugins. Which you will choose will depend on your needs.

Do you need something that posts your Wordpress posts in Twitter?

Do you need something that will take your Tweets and post them in Wordpress?

Or do you want something that will just display your Tweets in the sidebar of Wordpress?

There is no right or wrong answer here. It is entirely up to you how you want to use this functionality.

If you are stuck for which is best then Twitter Tools or Twitter for Wordpress are both good plugins.

To add a plugin to your Wordpress blog all you need to do is select Add New from the Plugin menu within your Wordpress administration panel.

Then in the search box all you need to do is type in Twitter and all the Twitter related plugins will appear.

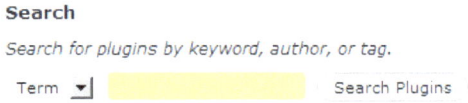

Each plugin will require some configuration but this varies from plugin to plugin. None of them are difficult to configure as they usually contain instructions and are intuitive. Most require little more than your Twitter user name and password!

Once you have your plugin installed and configured you will be have your Twitter account and your Wordpress integrated.

Harnessing the Power of Twitter

The default Twitter layout isn't exactly interesting and exciting to look at, is it?

Twitter has followed the lead of Myspace and decided to allow people to "pimp out" their Twitter account and change the background and the like.

If you are using this for business then this is actually a good idea to do because it will make your Twitter account stand out from the crowd.

Firstly, before you start this you should add a picture to your Twitter account. This may be a picture of you or it may be a picture of something related to the subject you will be Tweeting about. Which it is will be your decision based on your strategy and what you are planning on using Twitter for.

Some people will want their picture on their Twitter account because they are using Twitter to build up their reputation.

Others may be using a pseudonym and so not want their picture to be displayed or may just be using Twitter for SEO purposes.

Having a picture will help you to get followers following you because you will appear to be a real person (which obviously you are).

Go to the Settings menu and select picture to upload your picture to Twitter.

Maximum size of 700k. JPG, GIF, PNG.

Save

Note the maximum size of the file is 700Kb, which means if the file is bigger than this you either need to crop it or shrink the size.

Once you have added a picture, then you can set about designing your Twitter background.

Firstly though, a word of warning.

When creating a Twitter background please make sure you adhere to the standards of tastes and decency. Real people will be looking at your Twitter account and if the color combination makes them violently ill then they are not going to want to spend much time there and probably will not want to follow you.

Therefore please make sure your color scheme looks nice and is acceptable to the eyes.

When you go to the Design menu option, you will have the ability to change the theme and design for your Twitter account.

Firstly, you need to set the background image.

Select a **theme** »

Change **background image** »   Change design **colors** »

cancel   save changes

Twitter has some built in themes already, but you may not want to use them and may want your own, in which case you can select "Change background image" and upload your own file from there.

You can see here that the file must be smaller than 800KB and that you can set it so that the background is tiled if the image file isn't big enough to fit the whole screen.

You can either get a stock picture from a stock photography site or use one of your own here, it is up to you. Whichever you choose, make sure you have the rights to use it in a Twitter background and it isn't a copyrighted picture – you don't want to be getting into any trouble.

You can also change the colors of the background, text, links, sidebar and sidebar border, as per the above picture.

Clicking on any one of these will bring up a color selection box (shown below) from which you can choose the color you want.

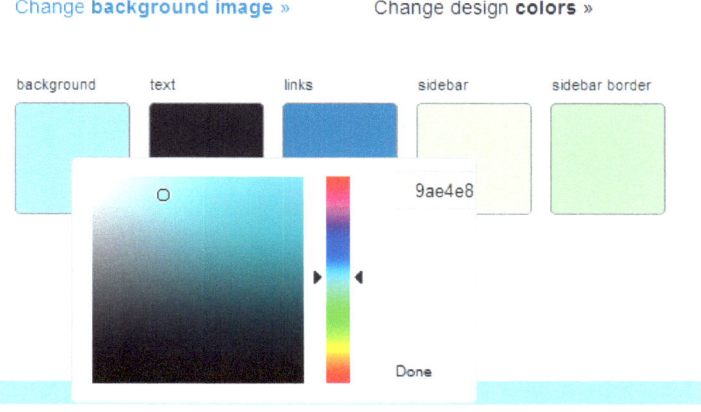

From this you can customize your Twitter account and make it completely unique.

There are designers out there who will offer you a custom Twitter design and charge you a lot of money (hundreds if not a thousand dollars) but you don't really need them.

Any designer who can create you an image to use or any piece of stock photography that is relevant will do.

Play around with the colors and the background and it won't be long before you have a really nice looking Twitter account.

This will get people's attention, make you stand out from the crowd and help you get followers. Not very many people are customizing their backgrounds significantly, so it is a good change to get some attention from your potential followers.

Twitter For SEO

You are not just limited to using Twitter for communicating with your followers. Twitter.com, like every other website gets indexed by the search engine spiders, looking for fresh food.

This is potentially incredibly valuable for you.

If you have a website that you want indexing quickly, then Twitter.com is a great way of getting it indexed. If you put links to your website in your Tweets then you will find that the search engines will follow them to see what is on the other end.

This means that you need to announce your websites in your Tweets so that they get the attention from the search engines.

There is a downside to this. If your followers consist of some of your competitors and rivals in your niche then they will be able to see exactly what products and services you have in your portfolio.

This could potentially open you up to be copied and get competition you weren't perhaps counting on.

You may want to have a different Twitter account with no followers in order to "announce" your websites to get the SEO benefits.

When posting URL's to Twitter, post the full URL in your Tweet. You then want in include some of your keywords around the Tweet. Make sure you write naturally as that is what the search engines are expecting from Twitter.

Make a few posts before and after your URL post that are related to that URL and include keywords. This takes advantage of what is known as Latent Semantic Indexing

(LSI) which looks for related keywords around a link to see how relevant the link is for the keywords.

Marketing With Twitter

Ultimately you want to make money with Twitter, and the ultimate goal is to build your business by marketing your products and services through its micro-blogging services and by building up a list of followers.

You are unlikely to make money directly from Twitter. You are more likely to make money indirectly, i.e. people go from Twitter to your website where they then sign up for a list and are sold to so you make the sale.

Twitter is not about marketing directly, it is about a much more indirect, subtle approach to marketing. You can't market here like you would with a sales or squeeze page. You have to take a slightly more softly softly approach and draw people in slowly.

You have to remember that Twitter is first and foremost a social network that has been co-opted into being a marketing tool. As such you market your products here differently to how you would traditionally market a product.

Twitter is an excellent tool for marketing and this chapter will give you some advice and tips on how to make the most from Twitter in order to maximize your effectiveness and profit.

Firstly, it is important you remain active on Twitter and Tweet daily at a minimum. Make sure all your Tweets are professional in their approach. Try to aim for 80% of Tweets to be related to your niche and 20% to be personal to build yourself up as a "real" person that people can trust and work with.

You don't have to Tweet constantly about your websites or blogs. Send people to articles you have written, to landing pages and so on. It works well to Tweet a teaser or two about an article and then point people to the article page.

Of course, this page is monetized in some way and probably also has a way of capturing their email address too!

The more informative and entertaining you are when you Tweet, then the more you will find your followers will listen to you and click on your links. You really do need to have a great personality to succeed on a service like Twitter. Let the personality sign through and almost be larger than life and you will find it much easier to market your products and services.

If you can tie your Tweets in with current hot and popular topics then you are more likely to get yourself noticed. This is because these topics are on people's radar and they are looking out for information on these subjects even if it is only sub-consciously. Therefore, when you post something on this topic it stands out to them.

You can create a squeeze page specifically for your Twitter followers to capture their email addresses. Naturally, you are going to have to offer them something of value in return for their email address.

You could tie this in with a service such as www.TweetLater.com so that all your new followers are sent a direct message (known as DM in Twitter speak) sending them to this squeeze page.

If you remember that Twitter is a social network and is about building relationships then you will do ok with your online marketing. Those who rush into Twitter like a bull in a china shop and expect people to drop everything to buy their products are the ones that fail to make any money from it.

By taking the time to cultivate personal relationships with your followers and to establish yourself as an expert you will be in the position where you are going to be able to make sales and drive traffic to your websites. Marketing with Twitter is entirely possible and you can make some good money from it.

The Future Of Twitter

The big question is … what will the future of Twitter be?

It is hard to say for sure, but its star is rising and it has become the latest site for the famous and fame hungry to hang out on.

Unfortunately for Twitter, just a few years ago, MySpace was the place to be. Last year it was Facebook.

Will it still be Twitter next year?

With a recent study stating that around 10% of users account for 90% of Tweets. Over 50% of people Tweet less than once every 74 days.

It does seem that Twitter is enjoying the benefit of its own hype and the hype generated by marketers and other big names. Whether it has the staying power to last out this hype and become a long term stable force in the social networking arena is yet to be seen.

The furore around MySpace and Facebook has died down somewhat, but they still attract massive amounts of traffic. Approximately 20% of global Internet users visit Facebook every day with it having an Alexa Rank of 4. MySpace fares slightly worse, but still has an Alexa Rank of 11 and 5% of global Internet users visiting it.

Twitter is likely to be around for the long run and once the hype machines have moved on to the next "greatest thing" it will be able to breathe a sigh of relief and return to focusing on building its appeal to visitors.

The canny marketer will see through this hype and take advantage of the popularity of Twitter to build their reputation and to establish themselves as an expert in their chosen field.

Whereas Twitter may not have as many users as Facebook or MySpace, it is still a very popular site with some very good uses to you as an Internet Marketer.

Through some thought and work you can enjoy many benefits from Twitter, particularly whilst the media hype lasts and it is rapidly increasing its user base. Now is a great time for you to jump on the Twitter bandwagon and enjoy the potential profits and notoriety you can gain from it.

Resources

http://www.WebsitesDesignLA.com/contact-us

http://www.SeoExpertDanny.com

http://www.SEO-service-inc.com/

44

ABOUT THE AUTHOR

Randolph M. Hirsch began his writing career in 2004 with his first feature length screenplay, Once In A Lifetime: "Just Go For It!" A Romantic comedy drama. He eventually condensed the screenplay in to a 20 minute short film, which he later produced and submitted it to the New York short film Festival, and it was very well received. Following that, he made two Travel Documentary films in 2006 and 2007, Randolph Hirsch Discovers Ukraine and Randolph Hirsch Discovers Paris. He later released a how to business guide for Accountants entitled: The Blueprints Marketing Guide for Accountants, Tax Professionals and CPAs. Recently, Mr. Hirsch has released six books in 2014: There's A Reason You're Here Moshe, Once In A Lifetime: Just Go For It! The feature screenplay, Daniel Day-Lewis, three time Academy Award Winning Best Actor, the Ultimate Biography, Philip Seymour Hoffman, Academy Award winning Actor of Capote and the Master, the Ultimate Biography of a Great Actor, Matthew McConaughey, Best Actor 2014: The Ultimate Biography, and Making Kids Smile, a how to guide for aspiring children's entertainers and performers. He is also re-releasing a newly re-mastered DVD version of his short film, Once In A Lifetime: Just Go For It, just as it played at the New York Short Film Festival ten years ago. He's currently finishing "The Boogie Nights Series." A Complete color photo Biography series of books about the director, Paul Thomas Anderson and his favorite actors and actresses from the film Boogie Nights, including Mark Wahlberg, Don Cheadle, Julianne Moore, William H. Macy, Burt Reynolds and Heather Graham, due to be released in May 2014. Randy lives in Los Angeles with his fiancée, one daughter and their doggie Bijou.

Books and DVDs by Randolph M. Hirsch

Philip Seymour Hoffman, The Complete Biography of a Great Actor, Memorabilia and Trivia Guide, April 2014

Daniel Day-Lewis, Three Time Academy Award winner for Best Actor, the Ultimate Biography, March 2014

The Blueprints Marketing Guide for Accountants, Tax Professionals and CPAs, 2011

Once In A Lifetime: "Just Go For It!" Feature length screenplay

There's A Reason You're Here, Moshe, January 2014 (Alternate title) The Ordeal: Best True Story 2014!

Matthew McConaughey: Best Actor 2014! The Complete Unauthorized Color Biography and Trivia Guide, April 2014

Making Kids Smile! A How To Guide for aspiring children's entertainers and performers

Randolph Hirsch Discovers Ukraine, Travel Film DVD 2007

Randolph Hirsch Discovers Paris, Travel Film DVD 2007

Once In A Lifetime: Just Go For It! Short film DVD version, re-released 2014

Cate Blanchett: Best Actress 2014! Color Photo Biography and Trivia Guide

Mark Wahlberg, The Ultimate Biography (Boogie Nights Series) May 2014

Don Cheadle, The Ultimate Biography (Boogie Nights Series) May 2014

Julianne Moore, The Ultimate Biography (Boogie Nights Series) May 2014

William H. Macy, The Ultimate Biography (Boogie Nights Series) May 2014

Paul Thomas Anderson, Biography (Best Director Series and Boogie Nights Series) 2014

Burt Reynolds, The Ultimate Biography (Boogie Nights Series)

Heather Graham, The Ultimate Biography (Boogie Nights Series) May 2014

Alfred Molina, The Complete Biography (Boogie Nights Series) May 2014

John C. Reilly, The Complete Biography (Boogie Nights Series) May 2014

Jennifer Lawrence: The Ultimate Biography (American Hustle Series)

Amy Adams: The Ultimate Biography (American Hustle Series)

Bradley Cooper: The Ultimate Biography (American Hustle Series)

Christian Bale: The Ultimate Biography (American Hustle Series)

Jeremy Renner: The Ultimate Biography (American Hustle Series)

KINDLE Gold Rush! How to write, publish and sell an E-Book on Kindle and Amazon

Twitter Power! Harnessing the immense power of Twitter to gain customers and profits

www.ingramcontent.com/pod-product-compliance
Lightning Source LLC
Chambersburg PA
CBHW040923180526
45159CB00002BA/587